The Locas

Carol Owen Reynolds

Jan-Carol Publishing, Inc
"every story needs a book"

The Locas
Carol Owen Reynolds
Published March 2025
Illustrated by Alexander Grayson Brown
Heirloom Editions
Imprint of Jan-Carol Publishing, Inc.
All rights reserved
Copyright © 2025 Carol Owen Reynolds,
Meta Francis Grayson, and Alexander Grayson Brown
Graphic Design by Tara Sizemore
Cover Image (flowers): © Karenfoleyphoto/Adobe Stock

This book may not be reproduced in whole or part, in any manner whatsoever without written permission, with the exception of brief quotations within book reviews or articles.

ISBN: 978-1-962561-68-6
Library of Congress Control Number: On file

You may contact the publisher:
Jan-Carol Publishing, Inc.
PO Box 701
Johnson City, TN 37605
publisher@jancarolpublishing.com
www.jancarolpublishing.com

This book is dedicated to my children, Shane Michael Grayson, John Scott Grayson, and Connie Grayson Criswell.

My children turned out to be successful, talented, and highly contributing members of society—in spite of me. Just like Him, my kids stuck with me through thick, thin, drinking, divorces, and finally my awakening to the real love of the Good Lord who passes all understanding. I love them to the max!

> As the opening words of every episode said,
> "The names have been changed to protect the innocent."
> — DRAGNET, *the television show*

Table of Contents

Numero

1	Uno	In Spanish, a "loca" is a crazy woman. Other Locas herein described are anonymous. You will have to figure out who they are, if you care.	1
2	Dos	Named me Loca Numero Uno. I named her Loca Numero Dos.	5
3	Tres	Friend from way back. Like, 82 years back.	10
4	Cuatro	ALWAYS there for me. I miss her every day.	14
5	Cinco	Listened to my troubles. Large laugh.	19
6	Seis	A relative. Not difficult to identify. Will be most interested in my description of her.	23
7	Siete	Also a relative. More difficult to identify.	31
8	Ocho	Walked in when others walked out!	35
9	Nueve	A psychic.	39
10	Diez	Fed us. Saved me when I was down and out.	46
11	Once	Intelligent. Strong sense of quiet humor. Miss her, too.	50
12	Doce	Good lookin'. Funny as a rubber crutch.	53
13	Trece	Lived to be 100!	56
		Acknowledgments	58
		About the Author	59

Numero Uno

"Friends are God's way of taking care of us."
— Author Unknown

Most of my friends are "locas." In Spanish, a "loca" is a crazy lady. I got the name from my friend, Loca Numero Dos (more about her later). My friends are all a few steps above that, but not by much! That's what I like about them. I didn't realize until just yesterday that I picked them, so they can't be too far gone, because I'm "lumped in with them," as my friend Loca Numero Once used to say.

The dictionary defines friendship as the cooperative and supportive relationship between two or more people. That's a pretty dry description of what friendship really is, I think. My description of friendship is "doing things and giving time and treasure to one another, not because we <u>have to</u> but because we <u>want to</u>."

Everyone has a story. By reading a story of my friends, you will be reading my story. Each story has its own time and space. This is not in time sequence. Each one is a standalone story.

I will be describing twelve of my friends, although it is a "short list" for now. There are also degrees of friendship that span over a lifetime. Some last a lifetime, and some are temporary. All are important, and all teach us something of value. Everyone knows that Numero Uno is me, Carol, but the names of my friends are disguised by number (numero).

Sometimes you will see "OUTCOME:" at the end of a story. It is because I felt it is relative to the story, but I didn't want to include it in the story, and I have tried to keep the stories lighthearted instead of negative.

I take a great deal of pride telling people I think I've sewed at least 1,000 things. I learned to sew in high school, where the teacher required us to go beyond what was sensible and make everything perfect. She started us out creating a perfect apron. Before graduating high school, I had followed a pattern, saving every inch of fabric, not necessarily saved on the pattern layout. I learned to match plaid fabric so that every line continued on, as if there was no seam involved.

I was the head cashier at a lady's dress shop in downtown San Diego and lived alone in a very small, formerly government-owned cottage on the corner of Park Boulevard and University Avenue. I took the bus to work, and my monthly rent was $40. When my future husband decided to move in, I asked the landlord how much and if my rent would increase after we were married. He said it would increase to $45. Although this seems a small amount for rent, you need to consider I was earning $47 cash a week. We moved to a larger house a couple of blocks away after my husband began working.

I sewed my own maternity dresses and began making my baby's clothes as soon as I discovered I was pregnant. There was a two-piece, black maternity dress I did *not* sew. I purchased it at the maternity shop on Fifth Avenue in downtown San Diego. This outfit was lined and very "dressy." The outer fabric was chiffon with a large ruffle around the top, covering a pink flowered pattern on the see-through bodice.

The dress was more than I could really afford at the time, so I put it on payments the minute I was told I was pregnant. We went dancing at the Lafayette Hotel nightclub and won first place in the dance contest two weeks before I lost our first child.

We, my first husband and I, had three more children thanks to a new series of shots every two weeks and in the fifth month, every week of my pregnancy. No, these shots weren't thalidomide, the shots that caused babies' deformities in the '60s.

All three other children are now in their late fifties and early sixties, all gainfully employed (thank you, Lord). I was a tough mom and never thought I was cut out for the job as Mother. I tried to make up for it in later life, and I hope my two grandchildren think I'm a more than a terrific grandma. Here's an example of my toughness as a mom:

TOUGH ON MY KIDS:

The timing was great when my daughter was a year old. The May Company at the Mission Valley Shopping Center had a special for studio pictures. She seldom gave me any trouble, but I knew she didn't like her picture taken unless it was a picture with her brothers. First of all, she had to sit alone on a propped-up table, and her stubborn nature took over. She reached for me, and I told her it was okay. I would be right close by, and it would only take a minute.

"Now, smile at the nice man with the camera!" I said. Her bottom lip pouched out and she reached for me again. She tried to get up and began kicking her feet. I could see my special price going down the drain. The cameraman did his very best to get a decent picture of her after several tries, but we ended up with an ornery pose and a frustrated mom (me).

I had to stop at Newberry's for a few things on sale before going home, and the line at the register was long. I didn't have her stroller and held her close, along with my few purchases. When it came time to pay, I had to stand her beside me to dig in my purse for the money. She immediately sat on the floor and again started kicking her feet. I told her to shut up and behave herself! One of the ladies behind me in line said to her friend, "Did you see how she treated that poor child?"

I picked her up under her armpits, shoved her in the lady's face and hollered, "Do you want her? You can have her!" The whole store went quiet, even my daughter. Time for a nap! End of story.

THE LAST 30 YEARS:

After marrying, divorcing, and trying to get my act together, I attended a Cursillo Weekend at the Catholic Conference Center in Julian, California. (It is called The Walk to Emmaus in the Protestant religion.) I ended up a speaker at a couple of weekends. It was the last talk of the first day, a personal witness talk.

When I was helping with dishes after my talk, a lady came up to me and asked, "Did your talk have anything to do with alcohol?" I told her it had, and she said, "My daughter heard your talk and said she would never take another drink!" I began a prayer life and participated in my Catholic faith since. My friend, Nueve, said she wondered if that old person would ever again come out. I'd say she does, but very seldom.

Numero Dos

*"A faithful friend is a sturdy shelter;
he that has found one finds a treasure."*
— The Book of Sirach, 6:14

First, it was, "Hey, Loca!" Then, it was, "Hey, Numero Uno!" Then, it was, "Hey, Numero Uno Loca!" Not to be outdone, I started calling her back, "Hey, Loca Dos!" Before I could spit out any more titles, we were hugging each other. That's my Loca Dos.

I first remember seeing her on her wedding day at St. Rita's Catholic Church, the little Spanish church in Southeast San Diego, 60 years ago. I remember thinking the groom was a lucky man, marrying into her family with seven children. The reception at Balboa Park in San Diego caused me to *rethink* that maybe she was lucky too. *Pretty ritzy*, I thought.

Loca Dos is from a family with good Catholic values, who works hard and believes the key to success is a good education — an upper education that her parents didn't get. She is what we called "a sensible person." Loca Dos is always upbeat and has the situation well in hand. The Catholic Church was the binding factor that kept the family upright and out of trouble.

You should not be surprised to see Loca Dos's mother answer the door with a bottle of bleach in her hand. Her mom's door was welcoming to others, and a meal was offered any time we surprised her with a visit.

Loca Dos's father was a migrant farm worker when he first came to the United States. That's why the children were all so healthy and lived to be elderly people; they had fresh fruit and vegetables every day. Later, he worked on the docks in San Diego, where he earned enough money to support his big family. He generally shared a meal with a person who could use a meal and who also appreciated his company, downtown.

A few years later, my family and I moved to Loca Dos's neighborhood, two blocks away from her home. My husband had started work as a law enforcement officer, so I was left alone at home during the night with our three children.

I had put the children to bed early and was busily writing letters to everyone, letting them know about our move to this nice neighborhood. The light was on at the dining area just inside the patio where I was writing my letters. Suddenly, someone shook the patio door handle, trying to get it open!

The first thing I did was run to the bedroom closet to get my husband's off-duty revolver. I thought, *Oh my God! What could an intruder do to my daughter?* I was not thinking straight enough that he might do the same thing to my sons. This was the first time in my life I realized I could kill someone.

Then, he began shaking the back door handle! I immediately called Loca Dos and her husband. She said, "We will be right over." By the time they got to the house, the door shaker had left.

I met Loca Dos's husband at the front door. As I held the butt of the gun in my hand, my palm was dripping with sweat. Loca Dos's husband calmly said, "Carol, put the gun down." I had it pointed straight at his midsection! He stayed safely inside with me while Loca Dos was driving around the neighborhood, looking for the door shaker.

After Loca Dos gave up her search for the door shaker, she returned to the house and called her two brothers, who I had never met, and told them to get over to our house to stay the night with the children and me. Her brothers' old pickup roared up the driveway, scaring away any prospective unwanted people in the entire Allied Gardens neighborhood.

The next morning when my husband arrived home, he came upon an old, dilapidated pickup in the driveway and two men sound asleep in the den. I hadn't slept all night and didn't even thank them or offer them breakfast.

Another time, early in the morning, Loca Dos had walked her daughter to the nearby preschool. Upon her return home, inside the side yard, she found four teenage boys going in and out of the garage door stealing beer from the garage refrigerator. Unafraid again, she scolded them, made them put the beer back, and told them to be on their way — that her husband would be angry if someone drank his beer.

Shortly after the teenagers left and were out of sight, Loca Dos decided to walk across the street to tell her neighbor, an off-duty policeman. He suggested that they drive around the area to look for them. Loca Dos ducked down in his car and peeked up as they drove. She spotted them a block away, lounging on the front lawn of a nearby house. She was very relieved when the policeman said he would take it from there. Loca Dos did not appreciate it when her plans for the day were interrupted by such nonsense!

Loca Dos is always aware of what's going on around her, especially when kids are present. She will notice what picture is being presented when children are in the area. An example of that could be Halloween night at Foster Elementary School. I got the bright idea to dress like a man, and I truly wasn't recognizable. I had dark glasses and a man's hat that helped cover my face. I nuzzled up close to Loca Dos and grabbed her behind. She spun around, made a fist, and would have decked me if I hadn't begun laughing. She didn't think it was funny. I guess I shouldn't have done it.

Square dancing was still big in the '70s. There were lots of big, gathered skirts and yards of petticoats under them. We joined the Dynamic 8s, just a few miles from our homes. Dale Durbin was our caller. What I liked about square dancing was that we had to listen to the caller and dance to his instructions, while showing off our beautiful costumes. We laughed so hard when the dance was over; some of us with weak bladders had to race to the bathroom.

I made dresses with yards and yards of gathered layers that matched our husbands' shirts. I even bought a special tool to put snaps on the men's shirts. I don't specifically remember making Loca Dos and her husband their costumes, but she said I had. So, I asked her, "When would I have had the time to make your outfits?" She replied, "At night when your husband was working because you couldn't sleep." I'd be awake all night until my husband pulled in the driveway, and I fell asleep before he cut off the engine. I guess it was a throwback from our incident with the door shaker.

Loca Dos has been especially supportive and proud of my transitional change in our Catholic religion. Some people call it a metanoia. She and her husband frequently attended Mass when I was the Reader (Lectora) at the San Diego Mission de Alcala. Her husband knew I was always a little nervous. Just before I started down the main aisle, her husband in the back row quietly said, "Don't screw it up!" Maybe this was payback for holding a gun at his midsection and grabbing his wife by the butt at the Halloween carnival.

Over the years, Loca Dos and her husband are spending their retirement near Vanderbilt in Nashville, where my current husband and I go for his yearly checkup for his heart transplant. He and Loca Dos enjoy preparing food and working in the kitchen, while Loca Dos's husband and I enjoy watching them!

Numero Tres

"Everyone hears what you say. Friends listen to what you say. Best friends listen to what you don't say."
— Author Unknown

She was my first friend and has to be on the list. She and I were friends from about the age of one and a half. Her parents owned a gas station and repair shop in Fessenden, North Dakota. When we went to town from the farm, we always stopped at the station, and our moms let us play in their apartment inside the big building that housed everything. Her story will be called "Numero Tres." Tres was born later in the year than me, and she was petite and bashful.

My parents bought a house in Fessenden, just a block down the road from Tres's parents' station. The biggest reason we moved to town was because my parents didn't want me to ride the speeder (railroad pump handcar) to school like my brother, who had been riding the speeder to school in town for a couple of years.

My brother walked to school with me the first day. We had been given strict orders from our mom to not "start fights." We didn't have preschool or kindergarten in those days, so I was six before I started school, being born in January. I asked my brother what I should do if anyone asked me my name, and he said, "Tell them it's none of their beeswax." I also think my brother didn't want to walk with me to school because he already had friends there, and I would have been too slow for them. Besides that, they probably didn't want to be seen with a girl.

I guess our mothers worked out very quickly that Tres and I should walk to school together. I would walk alone as far as the gas station and meet up with Tres.

Even though Tres was bashful, she gained a good deal of confidence about halfway into the first grade when the other students realized that she was the smartest one in our class. We were allowed to ask another student if we needed help with our work, and the kids would line up on either side of her desk until it got to be too much of a distraction when the teacher would make us sit down.

Tres and I were having a race down the sidewalk at school. I was beating her bad and laughing at her non-athletic abilities. I turned around just in time to hit one of the boys just slightly shorter than me. He had been looking around also and turned back just in time to hit me. My head spun and my nose still hurt days later. I found out years later that I have a deviated septum. Tres tried her best to comfort me, even though I had laughed at her. This is the mark of a true friend, I think.

Home Economics was for the high school girls. Time to learn to sew. One of the high schoolers made dresses to match for herself and her little sister. Unfortunately, the little sister had grown out of her dress and the fashion show was that afternoon. The teachers looked everywhere for a small girl, and bashful Tres was asked to wear the dress. She agreed, but only if I was in the fashion show with her. Both Tres's mother and my mother were called for permission to let us model in the show.

My mother didn't remember that I had worn a flour sack dress[1] that day. The ladies at Mom's morning coffee clutch the next day had a great laugh when she said, "I guess my homemade flour sack dress was in the fashion show yesterday!"

---

1 Flour sack dresses were frequently made from the 10-pound sacks of flour that were fabric, not paper sacks. Girls from rich families never wore flour sack dresses.

I was very protective of Tres, and we always discussed every move we made when we were together. It took until about the third grade for Mom to figure out why my dresses were always torn out at the waist on the left side. That was Tres's side. Still, I somehow thought it was okay for me to have other friends, but it wasn't okay for Tres to have other friends.

Tres was befriending another girl at a birthday party, and I quickly decided it was time for us to leave the party. I even faked illness, and we had to call Tres's mother to come get us from the party.

Then, that same girl tried to walk with Tres and me to school. I pushed her in a mud puddle, and she was forced to go back home and put on clean clothes.

It seemed like I could match Tres in at least one subject — Spelling — when we got into it in the third grade. Back and forth, we knocked out the others until there was just Tres and me left standing. It was my turn to spell HALLOWEEN. I was sure I spelled the word correctly, but Ms. Stensland said, "Wrong. Sit down."

Tres repeated the word and spelled it just like I had spelled it, and again the teacher told her to sit down. I was confused but happy Tres spelled it wrong, too. Then the teacher told us that we were both wrong because Halloween was spelled with a capital "H," and there were no winners that day.

Tres and I shared everything. We spent every moment we could together until about junior high school (now called middle school). We had our imaginary friends and "Brownie Scouts." The scouts were our own version of what scouts should be, and we called them "BS" meetings. For some reason, we weren't corrected for using that term. Maybe because our parents thought "BS" was too funny, so they let us use that term so they could have a good laugh.

We attended the Congregation Church, and honestly, if Tres hadn't forced me to go to church some Sundays, I probably would not have gone. I saw her family life as the model of what a family should be.

Nylon dresses and petticoats with yards and yards of skirts under them became the latest fashion. To make our dresses stand out even more, our mothers "sugar-starched" the petticoats.

Tres and I had almost identical dresses the first Easter after the new style came out, just in different colors. Tres and I had to hold our dresses down when we sat in church, and after a few minutes, the flies began buzzing around us. It took us a few minutes to figure out why the flies liked us so much. After all, we had taken our weekly bath the night before!

Tres always thought I was prettier and better dressed than she was, although I didn't agree. When we were seniors and it was prom time, my mother and I had gone to a great deal of trouble to remodel my gown from junior year by decorating it with sequins. Tres had begun to strike out on her own a bit, because she knew my family was moving to California after graduation. I was shocked to see her dressed for the prom. Her makeup and dress were perfect. She was beautiful! I told her later I wasn't prettier *that* night.

Tres did well without me. She finished college and began teaching in North Dakota, and later in Colorado, a total of 30 years in all. She met the love of her life, Oliver Bell, while teaching in Colorado Springs. Tres captured Ollie's story in a book called *Coming Up: A Boy's Adventures in 1940s Colorado Springs*.

Another of Tres's books also was a success, *Molly and the Cat Who Stole Her Tongue*. Besides being a cherished teacher, Tres has authored many, many articles in magazines and books, especially in the Colorado area.

Tres and I have been lifelong friends, and I cherish her with my whole heart.

Numero Cuatro

*"If you live to be a hundred,
I want to be a hundred minus one day,
so I never have to live without you."*
— Winnie the Pooh

Have you ever had a friend who would say, "Well, that was stupid!" Then, that friend would say, "Sit down. We'll talk about it. Do you want a scotch and soda?" That's the kind of friend I had in Numero Cuatro. She always told me the truth. I could say anything to her.

Children born in that era were allowed to play outside without adult supervision, and Cuatro's girls were no different, other than they weren't allowed to play or cross the street, but the sidewalk was okay. Shortly after our family moved into the neighborhood, Cuatro's girls came down to our end of the street. They ran home and excitedly told their mom, "We found some new kids at the end of the street!"

Cuatro always said, "You'd think they had found gold when they found your kids." I told her that they actually *did* and Cuatro just kept shaking her head to the contrary.

There was a swimming pool at Cuatro's house, and she allowed the local children to have swimming lessons, supervised and taught by qualified teachers. One of them was Numero Dos. We, too, were invited to swim at the pool, but strict rules were given about the supervision of the children. Cuatro could not swim, but when my daughter began to sink in the shallow end of the pool, Cuatro jumped in without hesitation to save her.

Cuatro stuck with me through many changes in my life, even though I'm sure there were times she was supportive when she probably didn't have time or patience to stick with me. She was a friend during my drinking days and my divorce days. She knew things about me that no one else has ever known. Cuatro wanted only the best for her friends but recognized betrayal for what it is. She said, "When I love, I love. When I hate, I hate."

I did not realize the value of "Salsa Night" at the time but realized later it was a women's support group and, thankfully, kept us sane. Especially me. We gathered at Diez's and Cuatro's houses mostly, and Cuatro was usually in charge of the main topic of the night, depending on who had the problem or major occurrence that week.

Cuatro was *not* shy, and when she had breast reduction surgery, she easily showed off her new "knockers" to us girls. It was a discouraging surgery because not only did it cost a lot, but also they soon returned to their old selves. I had a picture of four of us in a hot tub, she with her top lifted high, showing them off. Dang! Why can't I find that picture?

The new convenience of drive-up banking was introduced. Cuatro was having a bad day, and to add to it, she pulled too far away from the outside slot at the bank to deposit her check. She had to get out of the car and put in her deposit. A man in the car behind her honked his horn and said, "Hey, lady! You should pull up closer so you don't have to get out of your car." Cuatro yelled back, "Aw, shut up!"

Loyalty was Cuatro's greatest characteristic. She stuck with her husband even when she disagreed with him. He could fix anything. He wouldn't give up on anything until he figured it out. He had a bad heart that took his life, and for a year after his death, she didn't wash the sheets of his twin bed. She said she just wanted to smell his sheets.

After her husband's death, Cuatro sold their lovely home and moved into a modular home. She struck up a friendship with a volunteer at the hospital where she worked in the emergency room. She and her friend's relationship became serious after the death of his wife. Cuatro always said she only had two men in her lifetime.

When her "friend" turned 80 years old, Cuatro gave him a bang-up birthday party at a nice restaurant by the harbor. She paid for everything and invited their friends and our children. Her "friend" was old but still lively in the bedroom and ready at all times. Because Cuatro said she couldn't keep up with him, she bought him a blow-up doll and dressed it in one of her old, ugly dresses. He went along with the program and danced with the doll. It was a night I will always remember as one of our most fun.

Sometimes, several couples went dancing at the hotels in Mission Valley. It was the era of chiffon dresses and backcombed hair with lots of hair spray, of which I had both. Cuatro and I went to the bathroom. For some reason, women go to the bathroom together or in groups. I have always wondered why this is so for women, but not for men. Have you ever heard one man say to another, "Let's go to the bathroom?"

Anyway, when it was over, we were both washing our hands when Cuatro let out a scream! I asked her what was wrong, and she said, "Just look at yourself! You have your dress tucked into your pantyhose in the back!" After everything was fixed, and we were back to the table, she said, "I shouldn't have told you. I should have just let you get out on the dance floor like that!"

Cuatro had one of her surgeries at Grossmont Hospital. Nueve, another friend, and I went to visit her after having a few drinks. We asked the woman in the bed next to Cuatro's what kind of ivy that was in the plant her loved ones had given her. She said it was English ivy. A nurse came in at the end of our conversation and confused it with the IV (intravenous tube). She said that what was in the IV was none of our concern. We began laughing and more of the nurses came in to see what was so funny. All of us were laughing, except the first nurse who had gotten confused.

Then, I dropped my purse, and the contents flew all over the floor. This brought on more laughter and the charge nurse asked us to leave the hospital. Back in the car, I was driving. I was picking up my passengers in the parking lot, and when they reached for the door handles, I pulled a few feet away. And again, and again. More laughter. I could always say I had been thrown out of Grossmont Hospital.

Cuatro said she didn't go to the Catholic Church anymore because they kicked her out when she married a divorced man. I always felt bad about that, but she didn't seem to mind much. After I came to my senses and straightened up my life at a Cursillo – a method of Christian discipleship – I volunteered at the church and became a lector (lectora, as they called it at San Diego Mission de Alcala). I was running late one Sunday and had to drop something off at Cuatro's house.

When I ran in, Cuatro was busy baking cookies and had a piece of cookie dough in her hand. I said, "I just wanted to drop this off. I can't stay. I'm lectora today. I have to go." She turned toward me and cursed me, saying two bad words I can't put here. As long as I live, I will always have that image of her, standing there with the cookie dough in her hand and saying those two bad words.

Cuatro was very happy for me when I remarried but sad I was leaving San Diego. She was the maid of honor at my Catholic wedding. I had gained weight to where I was the biggest ever in my life. We knelt at the altar with our backs to the wedding guests for most of the Mass. Cuatro didn't hesitate to tell me that it "looked like I had two pillows stuffed in the back of my wedding dress."

After about a year, we went back to San Diego for a visit and rented a vacation home so we could entertain our friends. The morning we were set to leave, Cuatro brought over one of her jackets to be sure I was going to be warm, because now we had some snow in the winter. She sprayed the jacket with her perfume and threw it on the porch without knocking because she couldn't say goodbye again.

OUTCOME:

Cuatro's two men preceded her in death. She had four back surgeries and was in pain for many years. She couldn't find a reason to live, so she took her own life. I think of her every day of my life and will miss her until I can join her in the next dimension.

Numero Cinco

*"If at first you don't succeed, try again. Then quit.
There is no point making a fool of yourself."*
— W.C. Fields

My friend, Numero Cinco, was known for her large laugh! I think she laughed every day of her life with someone, someplace. She communicated with every person in her world, one way or another. She talked to people in the restaurant, in her home, at work and in the street. That's where I met her: across the street, in front of our house in the new-to-us Allied Gardens home. She was talking to another neighbor by her car. I had not met either of the neighbors, nor anyone yet in the neighborhood.

My four-year-old son was watching television in our den while eating some lemon drops. I was sewing in the same room, and the sewing machine faced the street where I could see the two ladies talking. Suddenly, my son started to choke on the lemon drop. The first thing I did was yell at him to, "Knock it off!" He was, and still is, the comedian in the family and would do anything for a laugh, so I thought it was another of his jokes to get my attention.

He choked again, and I got up from my sewing and looked hard at him. I slapped him on the back and still no response. I slapped him a second time on the back, and he gagged a little, but the lemon drop stuck. Then, I remembered it was right to turn him upside down and slap him on the middle of the back but not to reach in his mouth because it could push the obstruction even further down his throat. I tried that maneuver. It didn't work. By now, he was turning red, spitting and gagging.

I continued holding him upside down and ran across the street with him. I yelled, "He's choking!" Numero Cinco stopped talking, reached in his mouth, popped the lemon drop out that fell on the street. I continued to hold him upside down and ran back in the house with him still upside down. I didn't thank her or introduce myself. She continued with her next sentence and ignored us as if we didn't exist.

A few days later when I saw her come home from work, I invited Numero Cinco to our house and offered her a drink. I told her I wanted to thank her for saving my son's life. She asked if I had any scotch, and fortunately I had scotch and asked her if she wanted anything to go with it. She said she liked club soda, but I didn't have that, so she took it with a little water.

After a couple more visits to our house, Cinco invited me over for a drink after she got home from work. We slowly began to know each other. I thought it was interesting that she had heart surgery when her oldest son was just a baby. She had a hole in her heart the size of a silver dollar that was repaired at the University of California hospital in Los Angeles. She stayed in Los Angeles several days and missed her young son when her husband visited her on the weekends.

One weekend when her husband arrived for a visit, Cinco began to cry. He asked her why she was crying and she said she missed her baby. He didn't say a word but left Los Angeles and returned to San Diego to get their young son so she could see him. I thought that was one of the most loving things I had ever heard.

Cinco's children became fast friends with my children, especially her young daughter who was a year older than my daughter. They played Barbie dolls for hours. They built a big Barbie house in the extra back bedroom at their house. While playing dolls one day, the girls heard noise next door and remembered the occupants were at work. The girls sneaked outside to verify if, indeed, there were people inside drinking beer and playing pool. The girls told Cinco, and when the police arrived, the pool players had escaped out the back door.

We visited Cinco's mother, who ran a home for about four or five elderly ladies. Sometimes, they called it an "old ladies' home" or a "foster home." Other times, we went to the Lafayette Hotel Restaurant with her mother when she could get someone to sit with the old ladies. There was a piano player at the restaurant, and Cinco's mother would often sing along with the piano player.

Cinco's mother was devoted to her children. She would not attend any function if her children were not invited. She said, "If it's good enough for me, it's good enough for my children." Cinco's mother eventually came to live with Cinco's family in that back bedroom, and I would listen to stories of her life.

One of Cinco's mother's stories was about the time her husband caught another man making a pass at her. Her husband, fortunately or not, had on only a T-shirt and undershorts. He began to choke the man while holding him over the kitchen sink. She tried screaming for him to stop choking the man, and she tried to pull him off to no avail. Finally, she grabbed her husband's private parts and twisted them until her husband let loose the poor man. I'll bet the man who made the pass at Cinco's mother didn't do that again!

My husband and I went dancing and drinking whenever we could. This combination sparked romantic feelings. On the way home, I decided to start the teasing process before we went in the house. He decided we wouldn't wait, and just after he pulled in the garage, he told me to get in the back seat of the car. He closed the garage door, and we had a wonderful time. Actually, one of the best times I can remember. When we put ourselves together and opened the garage door, there sat Cinco's oldest son and his friends on their front lawn. They clapped, laughed, and cheered while we rushed inside our house.

Cinco loved watching *Wheel of Fortune* and *Jeopardy* on television. It always amazed me that she knew most of the answers before the contestants. She was another of my "brainy" friends who I thought could achieve more in life than the jobs they held. Not that being a bookkeeper for a large chain of grocery stores was a small feat.

Cinco loved the horse races and frequently attended the races at Del Mar, California. It was of little interest to me, but I would give her a couple of dollars to bet for me. One year, my brother had a horse running at Del Mar, and he was interviewed on television. I missed the interview, but Cinco thought it was great stuff that she saw the interview.

Fiercely independent, Cinco always paid her own way and knew she could get along in life to the very end. The last time I saw her, she was standing by her side gate, waiting for me to come visit. There she was, alone but aware she had begun to fail. She remembered I liked to drink scotch and soda with her. Sometimes, I wished I had taken the drink, but I had given up on it, and so had she. She got a phone call from her child while I was there, just checking up on mom...

Numero Seis

"Speak the truth, but leave immediately after."
— Slovenian Proverb

Another good quote that describes my sister would be from *Think Again* by Robert Anthony: "We are the people our parents warned us about!" She certainly thinks that way in her older life. Not so, when she was a tiny girl, coming home from a visit with our mother's friends at the coffee shop in Fessenden, North Dakota. Numero Seis cried, "The ladies didn't say I was cute today!"

Seis was blessed with clear blue eyes and blonde curls that snapped back against her head until later, when the curls wound around Mom's finger and fell perfectly in place. She had milk white skin and a pretty face. I felt like I had been kicked out of the "favored spot" and was left in the back row of the big audience Seis created. Even though Mom said she never had a child she didn't want, it made no difference to me.

Mom sewed Seis a coat from one of her own slightly worn fur coats. She would bundle Seis up and stuff her in the old orange crate that was nailed to the top of the sled and trudge to town, about half a mile away, for morning coffee at the Connor Hotel Café.

Mom was one of the ladies in town who first wore slacks. Not snow pants under the skirt, but real ladies' slacks. *Red* slacks! In addition to her slim, perfectly structured body, Mom had a beautiful face, too — a face like that of Numero Seis. Can you question why I was jealous of this duo?

Mom and her youngest sister even made a photo album of Seis's pictures and captioned each picture with cute sayings below each one. I was so insanely jealous, I made an album of my pictures with captions. I don't think anyone ever looked at the album except me. Today, I still have the album, but the jealousy is gone and I love the pictures.

Saturday nights belonged to Mom and Dad. It belonged to everyone in town, except the kids, who had to be home by dark. I had to *not only* be home, but I had to babysit my sister. The good part was that I could turn up the radio full blast and listen to the latest music while we danced around the dining room table. What fun we had dancing to "Rock Around the Clock" by Bill Haley & His Comets. Seis could be herself and admire me for who I was as her only friend during those evenings.

Seis seemed to be ahead of everyone in her classes at school. She was smart and even a little shy. Her teachers told Mom she was cooperative and intelligent. Our Mom and Dad had separated and were in the process of a divorce. Things at home were sometimes stressful, and Seis threw herself into her books. Today, Seis still finds her solace in books and volunteers at the library.

After Mom had married her second husband and gave birth to our second brother and Mom's fourth child, we moved from North Dakota to San Diego, California. Seis was about 11 years old. I jumped around from a couple of jobs, and at one point went back to live with the family for a few months.

The family moved to Saugus, California, after I married my first husband, but I stayed in San Diego where my children were born. We were struggling financially but had great friends, and I was able to be a stay-at-home mom. We lived in an old two-bedroom rental house. The floors weren't completely level, and if the children spilled their milk in the dining room, it ran into the kitchen.

Seis had come to stay with us briefly but returned to Saugus to be with the family. She went to school in that area but wanted to come back to finish high school in San Diego. Seis graduated near the top of her class at San Diego High but refused to go to graduation ceremonies to get that coveted "piece of paper" because our parents weren't coming to the ceremonies.

Our oldest brother, Seis, and I got the news that our father in North Dakota had died of cancer. Seis and I decided to go back for his January funeral and our brother would pick us up at the airport in Bismarck. The airline booked our flight, but we were on "standby." Sure enough, when we got to Denver, we were told we would have to spend the night in Denver and our luggage was on the plane headed for Bismarck!

Seis told me she was going up to the desk and she was going to tell them off. Thinking I should back her up, I followed her to the airline desk, and Seis asked the attendant, "What the hell are we supposed to do? Sleep in our underpants?"

We rode the airport bus into Denver and stayed at the YWCA that night. On the way to the Y, Seis asked me, "How did you know we'd stay at the Y?" I told her it was because I had thought it through, and that was probably the cheapest place in town. I did forget to call our brother and tell him we weren't going to be on the first plane coming into Bismarck, so he had to make the 117-mile one-way trip twice.

Seis asked me several times when we were going to the funeral home. She didn't remember what our father looked like because she was so young when we left Fessenden. He had lost a good deal of weight and even so looked remarkably good after a tough battle with cancer.

It was a beautiful service at the Congregational Church with standing room only. After the reception, Seis asked me who "Annie" was, and I told her she was a caregiver. Seis said, "I heard one lady ask another if our dad and Annie were having an affair." Only those who remember these two people will know why it is so funny!

The day of the funeral, it was six-below zero, and that night, it was 20 below. We didn't have the "wind chill factor" in those days. Also, in those days, bodies were not kept to be buried in the spring. The few who showed up for the burial were shaking from the cold. I remember it felt like my feet were bouncing off the snow beside the grave. After the funeral in Fessenden, Seis decided to return to Saugus briefly.

The family showed up for what I thought was a friendly weekend visit, but it wasn't friendly. Seis didn't talk. Seis was pregnant! Seis wasn't married! Seis had to call the father of her unborn child so he could come over for a confrontation, and he should "do the right thing." When the prospective father showed up, he was surprised, gainfully employed, and said he wanted to marry Seis. The big problem wasn't the unplanned pregnancy. The problem, as our parents saw it, was that Seis said, "I don't want to marry him!"

The family decided to leave Seis with us. I don't remember Seis complaining about her pregnancy, and she was willing to help with the housework and our three children, even when I did my exercises with my new "Mark Eden bust developer." The bust developer never worked, and I eventually disposed of it in the trash.

When the day came for Seis to deliver her baby, we took her to the nearby Catholic hospital. My husband went back home to tend to our children, and I occupied a seat in what they called the "fathers' waiting room."

The doctor reported that I was the proud aunt of a healthy baby girl. My niece was, and still is, one of the "apples of my eye." It was time for Seis to leave the hospital a couple days later, and the hospital staff said that Seis could leave, but they would not release our niece until the bill was paid. We borrowed the money from the credit union and brought them home.

We grew close to my niece, and she stayed with us off and on the next few years. While living in Oregon, Seis was to find out nine years later that our niece was diabetic. That was the day Seis grew up. I asked her what she was going to do, and she said, "We're going to take care of it."

There were many happy times, even though we lived away from one another. I attended my niece's graduation and wedding in Oregon. Seis, my niece, and her new son attended my second wedding. I tried each time I visited our aunt in Eugene to get together with Seis and my niece.

Our Mom in Billings, Montana, was in her eighties and beginning to have some health problems, so Seis and I decided it would be great if I could drive to Oregon, pick her up, and we would travel to Billings to pay Mom a visit during the time our other aunt from North Dakota was going to be there. Oh, what fun it would be!

And it *was* fun. Our North Dakota aunt told us about the many times she and Mom traveled and visited family. Mom needed to have her hair and nails done at the senior home where she lived in her lovely apartment. She took her shower carefully, got dressed up nicely, and started down the hall with her walker.

A couple minutes later, there was a knock at the door. I opened the door, and there stood Mom with her walker, announcing, "I. HAVE. SHIT. MY. PANTS!" It was like she was making the opening announcement for the start of the United States Congress. We did *not* laugh. I told her to get in the bathroom and I would help her get cleaned up from the waist down. In the bathroom, too, was our North Dakota aunt and Seis.

Mom stood in the tub, and I began washing her from the waist down. Our North Dakota aunt shook her head and left the bathroom. Then, Seis started to cry and also left the bathroom. Mom did not cry, but her voice broke and she said, "I hate to have you do this." I said, "Mom, you did it for me."

A few days later, Seis and I set out for our Oregon aunt's home in Eugene. It would be a long drive, but we were well prepared with food in our little ice chest and enough water. We decided to take the more southern route through Boise, Idaho, because we wanted to avoid any inclement weather. We did have great weather as we traveled south on Highway 15.

After a couple hours of travel, we saw a highway patrol sign saying we could expect a traffic jam 45 minutes ahead. Well, I thought, by the time we get there, it will be cleared. I thought. Two more signs, evenly spaced, warned us about the traffic stopped ahead. It seemed impossible because it was a lovely moonlit night, and we could see no traffic ahead.

And there it was! Cars and trucks lined up for miles! There was a small town to our left but no way to get to it. Then, I announced I had to pee. Seis asked where I thought I could pee if I couldn't get to that little town. I said, "If I have to, I'll pee in that little ice chest. Maybe you can reach back and start taking the food out." We were trapped with cars on Seis's side and behind us. In front of us was a big truck and trailer.

I told Seis to get out of the car and signal me when the couple in the car beside us wasn't looking. I was going to have to pee outside in front of the car. I couldn't wait any longer. I yanked down my pants and underpants and peed out a solid stream just as the truck driver came around the back of his truck to probably do the same thing. I told him, "I'm sorry you had to see that!" Seis laughed hard and threw her arms over the top of the front hood of the car.

We continued on, and after a couple hours, stopped for a small meal. Our waitress at a café in Sisters, Oregon, suggested maybe we could consider staying overnight there because McKenzie Pass could be rough and sometimes even closed during rough weather. Seis's face fell, and she looked at me for reassurance about the trip. I told Seis not to worry. I had done a lot of traveling, and it would be fine. When we got to the car, Seis asked if maybe we should rethink our plan. Again, I reassured her that I knew what I was doing, and besides that, people panic when they hear about a storm that may not even occur.

The night was cool, dark, and quiet. When we started into the area of the pass, a few flakes of snow fell. The lanes were narrow, but I was keeping up with the traffic on the two-lane road. As the snowfall began to pick up, the lights from oncoming traffic were beginning to blind me. The edge of the pass was on Seis's side of the car. Then, the snow picked up speed, and I told Seis to roll down her window halfway and be sure I wouldn't go over the side of the pass.

This was working out okay for us, but not for the cars behind us and cars from the oncoming traffic. I guess I must have forgotten to dim my lights, and everyone was tooting their horns at us.

It seemed like an eternity by the time we reached the bottom of the pass, and Seis was able to put her head back inside the car. Just as in the times we helped my sister, she didn't complain but became quiet and usually asked questions later.

We agreed we wouldn't tell our Oregon aunt what happened. She was waiting nervously when we arrived late at night, and we assured her everything went smoothly.

Numero Siete

"Friendship is one mind and two bodies."
— Confucian Philosopher Mencius

When I met Loca Siete in San Diego, she had just married my husband's brother. She had been divorced from a musician with one big hit, "Alley Oop," in 1960. Loca Siete was a shapely blonde beauty previously employed at the first factory manufacturing the latest rage, the "Baby Doll" pajama. The Los Angeles Rams toured the factory, and Loca Siete modeled the new style pajamas.

Uncle Mack took one of the first pictures of Siete and me. Just as he was about to snap the picture, Siete held up her hand and said, "No, not yet." She changed her position to my right side, carefully posed, and said, "This is my best side." Uncle Mack turned his back to us, bent over, and said, "This is *my* best side!"

Siete brought with her a son and therefore had a head start on her family. She, her new husband, and son made a handsome family. I was fair skinned and dyed my hair red at that time. I weighed 118 pounds. I thought I was fat!

When Siete became pregnant with her second child, she was thrilled and wanted to show her belly as soon as possible. She purchased a new maternity top and paraded up and down Texas Street, showing off her new top. A car with teenagers passed by, and one of the boys shouted out the window, "Hey, lady! Did you swallow a watermelon seed?"

Before we married into their family, the men made it clear they were obliged to support their "Mom" who lived in Guadalajara, Mexico. Even when we had our own children, Siete with four and three for me, we faithfully sent Mom a monthly check.

Our husbands had another brother in the Navy, unmarried at the time, and we came up with a plan to bring Mom to the United States so she could be taken on as his dependent, although we would still kick in support if needed. My husband was her youngest son.

Mom had become increasingly weak with a bad heart, and it would be a task, but we were determined to move her to the United States. I had kept a steady correspondence with Mom. She loved my letters, even though she sometimes had to have help deciphering them from her friends who could write and speak English.

After several months, lots of juggling and expense, we were able to move her as far North as Tijuana, Mexico. She stayed with her distant family members there, and I couldn't wait to see her. When I walked in their house, Mom opened her arms wide and said, "My daughter, my daughter!" Our efforts had made everything worth it for that one moment.

Mom had to rent her own place in Tijuana for a short time because she didn't have all the correct paperwork. We went back and forth many times and spent hours of time and expense to finally get permission to move her to our country. We packed the trailer as tight as possible to keep all her treasures. When we got to the border, the Border Patrol Officer told Siete's husband to unpack everything so he could inspect the contents. Siete's husband came back to us, following him in our car, and said, "I'll try to pay him off!" He talked a long time to the officer and slipped him about $60, and we were on our way!

Mom stayed with Siete's family for a short time but wanted her own place, so we found a small apartment close by and again went over her many papers for her residency and stay in our country. Mom didn't do well alone and called her sons many times to come see her, even late at night. The person who could muster up the patience and endurance with Mom was Siete, who could sit near and talk to Mom for hours until everything was okay with Mom.

Then, another snag in our plan stopped things for a short time. There had to be a sponsor for Mom with at least $6,000 in the bank at that time. (Currently, about five times that amount.) My father had recently passed, and I inherited enough to cover that amount, so we made arrangements at the Border to have her paperwork checked and a physical examination completed.

Mom had been reared in a strict, conservative, Catholic family and was dreading the physical pelvic examination, but she was willing, at this point, to do whatever it took to gain residency. Siete and I were nominated to take Mom to the Border because her sons were all working, and Mom wanted the women with her because of the dreaded pelvic examination.

We loaded up Mom early in the little red 1962 Rambler and left for Tijuana. Siete and I wore dresses and high heels to make a good impression. We waited three hours for Mom's appointment because the lines for the pelvic examination were long, especially with the lady doctor. Finally, it was Mom's turn, and the examination was over in a few minutes. I asked her how it went. She waved her hand and said, "It was nothing. She just quickly looked!"

Mom had what I called a "plethora of paperwork" in her purse that she clutched tightly to her chest. Surely by now, the rest of the day would go like the pelvic exam, but not so! We were one piece of paper short! No matter how hard we dug through the treasured papers in Mom's purse, the magic paper didn't show up.

So, I asked the agent in charge what we had to do to get the magic paper, and he said, "Well, you could get it today if you want to go to the Mexican Consulate in Tijuana. It's about 12 miles in." He chuckled and walked away. I knew my face was as red as my hair and I told Siete, "We're going. We aren't taking Mom. She's staying here with the doctor, and we are going to Tijuana!"

We jumped in the little Rambler and took off for the Mexican Consulate. We got about halfway into Mexico and the car began to shake. I got out and saw that the left front tire was flat. There weren't many people around, except for a few men standing together in the shade and watching us about a block away.

After half an hour of standing in the hot sun, a small boy about seven years old walked up to us and said, "Fix tire?" I asked him, "How much?" He said, "Two dollah." I gave him two dollars and he left, rolling my tire in front of him. Siete asked me what I was going to do if he didn't come back. I told her I didn't know, but I had no other choice.

About two hours passed, and the young boy came back with my tire. He put it on my car. We shook hands and I thanked him. We left for the Consulate. We got the treasured magic paper. We raced back to the Border, squeaking by just short of closing time.

OUTCOME:
Mom's heart gave out before she was able to gain her residency, and she died in the arms of her youngest son. Siete passed in 2019.

Numero Ocho

*"A real friend is one who walks in
when the rest of the world walks out."*
— Author Unknown

It was unusual for anyone to knock on my back door because we had a fenced in back yard, and behind that was a two-story apartment house. There she was! Holding a small baby girl in her arms and introducing herself. They had rented a place, not far away, but it had bugs and Numero Ocho hated bugs. So, they had left and rented the lower apartment behind us.

I invited her in, and she became a lifelong friend. Ocho had the typical East Coast/Boston accent. She was born and raised Catholic. She had been an emergency room nurse and fell in love with a sailor, stationed nearby. Her husband was now stationed in San Diego.

About four or five of our neighborhood ladies had our Coffee Clutch, even though she preferred tea. We let our children play in our back yard, because it was fenced in, and we could see the children easily. It was a constant vigil, checking on the children to make sure they were okay and getting along without fighting.

My oldest son was three years old by then and kept trying to climb the side gate. I was changing my daughter's diaper, when suddenly I heard the screeching of the brakes on a Lucky Lager beer truck. My son had made it over the gate and found his way to the street. The driver had him by the underarms and was screaming, "Where is your mother? Where is your mother?" I froze, and then kept changing the diaper. The driver put him over the fence and rushed back to his truck. Both Ocho and I blamed ourselves for not watching more carefully.

We had little money to afford expensive entertainment for the children, but we would take the children to the bay or to Balboa Park for a picnic lunch. Before giving them a bath, when we returned home, I would rinse the sand off my children outside with the water hose. A yellowjacket grabbed ahold of the bottom of my foot and began driving his stinger in my foot. Ocho ran to me and brushed off the yellowjacket, then began digging the stinger out of my foot. When I screamed in pain, she told me to shut up and stop being a baby!

We had plans to go to the drive-in movies on my husband's day off. We would hang a big blanket over the front seat and make the children hide under it in the back, so we didn't have to pay for them. Early that morning, I had pain in my left side. At first, I shrugged it off, thinking it may be the start of my monthly cycle. About 10 a.m., I told my husband I was going to have to go to the doctor because the pain was now too much to bear.

When the doctor examined me, he told me to go straight to the hospital. He said I had a twisted ovarian cyst about the size of an egg. He said it was filling fast and could burst. Against the directive of the doctor, I went home instead and began crying when I hit the front door. I said, "I have to go to the hospital, and I need to call my mother." My mother lived in Los Angeles, and I don't know why I thought she could help me.

Ocho, now very pregnant with her second child, came running through the back door and said, "Don't worry about a thing. I'll take care of the kids (and your husband). Just get to the hospital." And she did just that. She fed and bathed the children and even continued helping with them even after I returned home a few days later. The cyst the doctor removed was the size of a cantaloupe! I could not lift my daughter in her highchair, so every time she ate, Ocho would come over and help me.

We did everything for each other. When Ocho had her second child and her set of fraternal twins, she went back East for their births. I would unpack her things so she wouldn't have to do it with new babies in the house. Ocho and her husband bought a new home in Santee, California, and had a ton of things to unpack. Our mutual friend, Nueve, helped me a couple of times on her day off from Sears. Ocho's husband was going back and forth, trying to help and get things ready. The new neighbors watched us but didn't have anything to say.

Ocho and her husband had driven across the United States with their hatchback Barracuda. They drove up in our driveway first, because they were going to have a meal and pick up the keys to their house. The twins were asleep in the back of the slanted area of the car and the two older girls were in the back seat.

When Ocho stumbled out of the car, she was almost unrecognizable from exhaustion. It took a couple weeks before she could recuperate from the trip. Ocho's new neighbors told her later that they had wondered which of the women in her house was her husband's wife.

Our friendship was always constant, and we had many good times, as we were able to increase our lifestyles. Eating out had been a luxury. Now, we could even take the two families to the Chuck Wagon for Thanksgiving dinner!

When it was finally time for Ocho's husband to retire from the Navy and he returned home to an airport near their home in Boston, he proudly put his Navy uniform on for the last time. At the airport, someone called him a "baby killer." He had no idea what they were talking about. There was a myth and misconception that during the Vietnam War, some babies were killed in a United States raid.

Ocho and I corresponded and spoke to one another by phone. We could talk for hours. When I moved to Virginia, I did get to visit Ocho and her husband one last time.

I always felt Ocho was a pure soul. She had a long list on a sheet of paper of the people she prayed for each day. My family and I were on that list until she died.

Ocho became ill on a flight returning from her daughter's home in Ireland. A nurse aboard the plane told her to make an appointment with a doctor when she got home. She had all the signs of cancer. That nurse was right. Thankfully, Ocho claimed she wasn't in very much pain when she died. I often wondered if she truly did suffer much pain but was trying to make others believe she was okay. Ocho passed in July 2016 surrounded by her family and a picture of my daughter and me on her nightstand.

Numero Nueve

*"If you should die before me,
ask if you could bring a friend."*
— Stone Temple Pilots

Numero Loca Nueve first appeared in my San Diego world when she moved next door with another family of four from New York. Nueve brought with her a young daughter.

Most of the neighbors were renting their homes in our area, and besides watching television we couldn't afford much, except to visit and drink coffee. Some people called them "Coffee Clutches." My Coffee Clutch was composed of about four of the nearby neighbors. I had three children by now, so we met mostly at my house.

Before leaving New York and losing a baby boy, Nueve suffered from a ruptured naval. It accentuated her belly and was the target of much ridicule with the Clutch. We sometimes walked around the block at the suggestion of Nueve. Sometimes we would cut across the busy, commercial University Avenue, parallel to our Essex Street homes. Nueve thought that she would apply for a job in the credit office at Sears and Roebuck, just up the block from University Avenue.

Traffic was heavy and Nueve led the rest of us across the street. One of the drivers honked his horn and was forced to hit his brakes, avoiding Nueve. She turned, made eye contact with him, and said, "You can't hit me! I have a ruptured belly button!"

Nueve did get a job in the credit department at Sears, and her roommates were perfect babysitters for Nueve's daughter. It wasn't long before Nueve got her own apartment, close by, and met a man she eventually married and who adopted her child. After her daughter was adopted, she said to him, "Now you're my real daddy, huh?"

Nueve revealed to the Coffee Clutch that she had put ads in an offbeat newspaper saying she had psychic abilities. She had gotten a request from a woman in South America for her to remove a curse from an angry relative. A dead chicken was used to put the curse on her. Nueve replied to the ad that she "didn't do curses."

Numero Ocho brought a Ouija board to the Clutch. Simple questions like these were asked:
- Who will be able to buy a house first?
- Whose mother will die first?
- How many more deployments will Ocho's husband have to serve?
- Will my father-in-law really marry that new girlfriend?

When Nueve's predictions began coming true, it made believers of everyone, except one husband who called it "bunco." The ladies of the Clutch dismissed him immediately and told him the Clutch didn't include men anyway.

Most evenings, Nueve's new husband checked in at the nearby bar in Hillcrest. After all, it was good for business, and his friends from the Optimist Club showed up there too. They figured it was good for their businesses as well. Nueve thought she would see more of him if she matched him drink for drink but had to give up on the idea because she fell off the barstool. She just couldn't tolerate alcohol.

The local cop stopped Nueve's husband one evening on his way home from the local watering hole and asked her husband if he had been drinking and was told, "Oh, I had a couple beers at the Hideaway. That's all." The officer replied, "Well, maybe we should have you take a sobriety test," as he opened the car door and Nueve's husband fell out of the car. The cop quickly handed a drunk driving ticket to Nueve's husband and told him to park the car, because he was not allowed to drive home. When Nueve's husband looked at the ticket, he said, "I want a jury trial!" He was told he'd have to take it up with the court.

We were the first to buy a house, as Nueve had predicted, because my father had died and left me a small inheritance. Our locations changed, but the Coffee Clutch friends stuck together.

Nueve, her husband, and daughter decided to move to a big house about a mile away in East San Diego. It was bigger and had a lovely living room with a fireplace and long bookshelves on either side. Nueve tried to think of ways to get her husband home early for dinner. She called him at the bar and said she had a surprise for him when he got home. She decided to lure him by removing all the books from the top shelf of the bookcase, and when he came in the door, she was posing naked on the top shelf! He said, "Get down off there. You're making a fool of yourself."

My father-in-law did marry that new girlfriend. She was a member of the Socorro Club. Socorro means "to help" in Spanish, and the Club was charitable. She invited Nueve and me to a posh fashion show at the Catamaran, a beachfront hotel. Many prominent members of the community would be present and wearing long dresses. I was able to sew a long skirt with fabric I found on sale at the local Cornet five-and-ten-cent store. The skirt matched one of my blouses that was in good shape.

Nueve found a beautiful dress on sale at Macy's, but the dress was too long. Nueve was not a good seamstress and called me in a panic, saying she had her husband helping her shorten the dress. "Could you come over right away and help?" I rushed over and found her husband standing on a chair in the dining room, wearing the too tight dress. He couldn't get off the chair or out of the dress. We brought in a stool, helped him out of the dress, and I took the dress home to shorten it to fit Nueve. She looked lovely. He threatened to kill me if I ever told anyone about the long dress incident.

Not having enough drinks or enough strutting around in our new outfits, we decided to stop at the Hanalei in Mission Valley and graze the table for free fruit cups and a final drink. It didn't take long before we realized we were broke and had to buy a drink to justify the free fruit cup. I took Nueve home, and her husband was waiting on the front porch. We were laughing so hard, I accidently drove over the curb and onto the front lawn.

Unfortunately, Nueve's husband broke his leg and was incapacitated for a few weeks. He was having trouble keeping his leg in an upright position, so it began to swell. I came up with the idea to put a heat lamp on the cast. Nueve thought it was a good idea and promptly began heating it up. When he went back to the doctor because the leg was turning black, the doctor asked Nueve if she was trying to bake his leg in the shell!

Nueve and her husband loved to go swing dancing with us. He loved dancing more than she, I think. I always did my own pest control by spraying every other month outside around the house. Nueve's husband called one afternoon and asked my daughter (then about five years old), "Is your mother there? I'm calling to find out what time we are going dancing." My daughter said, "She can't come to the phone. She's cleaning the bugs out!"

Nueve's husband swung her around a lot and made a spectacular show on the dance floor. Sometimes, other dancers stepped back, applauded, and gave them the whole dance floor. She would circle him as he held her on one finger, he did the splits. My husband would say, "He's going to split his pants one of these days. I hope he splits his pants." He never split his pants.

The "jerk" became a new dance craze, and Nueve's husband combined that new move with the splits. While doing the splits and the jerk, he accidently came down too hard and broke Nueve's nose. Unfortunate, since Nueve had a metal plate taped to her nose when she was interviewing the public at the Sears credit department.

It was okay with Nueve's husband if he was getting the applause, but obviously not so if another man was getting the applause. Eighteen of us gathered, pushed tables together, and danced at Pal Joey's bar. We even took Nueve's mother-in-law to the bar located in this nice neighborhood.

The bar owner watched our tables and watched Nueve especially.

It was the era of go-go boots and hot pants for the young women, and Nueve looked just the best of our group in her new white boots. Nueve and her husband had another of their arguments, and when a young man from the next table asked her to dance, she accepted without getting permission from her husband. Getting permission from your partner was still an expected custom.

Nueve's husband watched them carefully and took all he could stand before he grabbed the front collar of her new dance partner and twisted it against his throat. He shoved the poor fellow up against our table. I picked up the candle and my half-finished drink before the table crashed to the floor. Pal Joey's owner asked our fighters to take their fight to the parking lot and he called the police.

Nueve's mother-in-law said, "She shouldn't have danced with him in the first place." Nueve quickly left with her mother-in-law in their car, leaving her husband to fend for himself. Her former dance partner jumped into a car with three of his buddies and left the scene. I was ready to go home. My husband, with all good sense, thought we should wait until the police got there in case the four men came back before the police arrived and finished off our outnumbered friend.

Nueve's husband refused to let us take him home, called a cab, and left. After what happened at Grossmont Hospital while visiting Cuatro, I told the owner of Pal Joey's I had been kicked out of better places than this!

The word got around town about Nueve's psychic abilities. Detectives knocked on Nueve's door and asked if she had any feelings about the killing of a local woman, because they were sure she was dead but couldn't find her body. Nueve asked them to take her to the park that overlooked a major freeway. Nueve's husband stayed in the car and shook his head in disgust at the idea that she should be asked, nor could she tell them anything anyway, he thought.

Nueve walked around the park for a few minutes, then stepped close to the edge overlooking the freeway and said, "She's down here. I can feel her. She's here."

A few days later, they found the lady's body just below where Nueve had indicated.

They needed to find water in a place called "New Hebrides," now the Republic of Vanuatu in the Coral Sea, east of Australia. Nueve said they looked for water all over the island, even using sticks with special powers, but could not find the water. She became dehydrated and when she got home, she pinched her skin, and it stuck together. The other housewives in the Clutch thought Nueve was our most interesting friend.

Nueve and her husband divorced, and Nueve literally fell into the arms of a man from Fort Worth, Texas. She passed out and when Nueve woke, the Texan said he remembered he had pulled her out in a past life from under a wheel. It didn't take long for that Texan to propose marriage and talk Nueve into moving to Texas with him.

The Texan owned a mansion with a colonial design on front and an English Tudor design on back. The mansion had an elevator that rose to the dance floor upstairs, but Nueve took the stairs to meet the Texan waiting below when they married at the mansion.

The government threatened to levy an unfair tax on the Texan's wine production, and the Texan moved all the wine to a field. He hired a friend with a bulldozer and invited the government officials, who had levied the tax, to the field. As the officials watched, he gave the signal to the dozer and destroyed all the wine. No product — no tax.

OUTCOME:

The Texan was swindled out of most of his money, and it struck him where Nueve said, "He couldn't fight back. With a cancerous brain tumor." Nueve, too, died of cancer. I was told she died in a whirlpool bath. I kept in correspondence with her to the end. I loved Numero Loca Nueve.

Numero Diez

*"A true friend never gets in your way unless
you happen to be going down."*
— Arnold H. Glasow

Numero Loca Diez was a friend first with Numero Cuatro. She was sitting by the pool in Cuatro's backyard. Her daughter was in the pool with the other kids. All of us were smoking cigarettes and watching the kids play Marco Polo. The game never made much sense to me. I couldn't see the point of some yelling "Marco" while others yelled "Polo" and then dipping in and out of the water.

It was too early in the day for alcoholic drinks, so we had to settle for Pepsi, served by Numero Cuatro. Cuatro always made it clear that we were not there to be served food and drinks. Only to swim. Most of the time, especially during the day, Cuatro did not offer anything, so we were lucky this day to have Pepsi. A large gathering/party at Cuatro's house was always prepared ahead of time and lots of total fun.

Unlike her friend Cuatro, Numero Loca Diez always served food. This was the Diez way of life. As I was about to find out, Diez's first question was always, "What are we eating?" Little did I know that I was about to embark on a whole new friendship journey with this beautiful soul.

Pool parties at Diez's place included a large crowd and more than enough food. Friday nights were special, though, and the Salsa Group was for the ladies. Every Friday evening, I would get a call to assure my attendance at "Salsa Night" at her house. Almost every time, I'd say, "I'm too tired and going to bed early." Diez would say, "No, you don't have to stay late. Just leave when you need to go to bed."

The Salsa Group nights usually wound up lasting until about 3 a.m. I thought later it was the best therapy session in town, although we didn't recognize it for what it was at the time. We would drink, smoke, and eat more than just salsa. The room was large, with a big table at one end and the living room furniture at the other end. If a husband or boyfriend showed up, he had to know his place and not interfere with our conversations. If any men came to Salsa Night, there was an unwritten rule that it was only the ladies at the table. If one or more of the men accidently sat at the table, it was at great risk to his manhood. The men would sometimes throw in a barb from the living room end.

Along came the era of the Chippendale dancers, and we couldn't be left out, although Diez and I had just gotten new jobs. About five of us girls went to see the male dancers at a bar in La Mesa. Oh, what fun we were having, even though we could only afford dollar bills to tuck in their waistlines! Some (not us) had the nerve to throw small change at them!

Suddenly, the front door of the bar opened, and the local news channel crew were filming before they even got through the door. Diez quickly backed up to a dark part of the bar, and I went back and asked her why she didn't want to be on the news. She said, "You dope! Don't you realize we could both lose our new jobs by being seen here?"

Diez traveled a good deal from offices all over Southern California in her work as a supervisor of the typing pools for escrow and insurance companies. She was on the ground floor of the computer work, but in a very special program designed for that company.

Diez had been widowed for a few years and had property in South Dakota. She was very industrious and could support herself, her daughter, and by now, a grandson. She rented one of her bedrooms to students from a nearby college. Sometimes, her renters would join in on our Salsa Nights but probably thought we were boring and old. We were in our forties.

Diez met a retired Navy man, who was recently divorced. He fit in well with our husbands and didn't mind helping Diez with her home and food preparations. When they married, it was a simple ceremony. I played the piano. Then, the party started! Big time! We had the biggest party of all at Diez's home, which included dancing. Diez looked the most gorgeous we had ever seen her. She was happy.

I was not happy. I felt trapped in a miserable marriage to my second husband. I had lost everything except my job. So, I got a divorce that took the very last penny I had accumulated, except my furniture and my '69 Corvette. Diez had a vacant room and offered me a place to stay until I could "get on my feet." Others said they would *not let me go to the street*, but it was *Diez* who offered me a place to stay.

I put my furniture and my Corvette in storage and started over. Diez treated me like a member of the family, and needless to say, she fed me well. After a few months, I started dating an engineer who lived in Riverside, California, so I was usually gone from Friday evening to Sunday evening.

OUTCOME:

Because of her love of Christmas decorating, her home was featured in the local paper at Christmas time. Diez's daughter died in 2020.

Numero Once

*"Knowledge is knowing a tomato is a fruit.
Wisdom is not putting it in a fruit salad."*
— A Paraprosdokian

A couple of my friends have what I call "a big brain." Neither of them ever said much unless it was worth saying. A lot of thought went into each thing they said. Numero Once was one of them. How she spent her time was worth everything to her. She was always working, learning, or doing — not that it was obvious to everyone, but I got to know it after I knew her for a long time.

It became necessary (I thought) to move to Riverside, California, when I was trying to fix a failed marriage, although I hadn't given up on him at that point. I just took any old job at an aircraft plant to keep us going. There, I met Once. She was friendly and accepting of me among new people.

Just for something to do, I would talk Once into going with me to the Swap Meet on Saturdays. My favorite shop was the Dollar Shop. Once thought it was a waste of money and time, but I loved it. I would stand in the middle of the little shop and point out to her, "Hey, look, this is only a dollar. There's all kinds of stuff here for just a buck." When she realized I wasn't going to leave until I bought something, she would come in the shop and watch me dig around the little piles of junk.

Once had a more prestigious job at the aircraft factory (bigger brain) than I had, so she was in an office with only three other people. I was a clerk with little responsibility, out on the floor in a cubicle with 100 other people. I *was* smart enough to know she was very conservative and would never reveal anything personal to a new friend. I called her on the office phone and asked her if she knew a good place in Riverside where I could buy a garter belt and fishnet hosiery. She couldn't suppress her laughter, and the others in her office were stunned.

Once had a new man in her life, but being the private person she was, wouldn't tell me anything about him except she did have a date once in a while. Finally, after several months of seeing him, she called me at my desk and told me who it was. Now, it was my turn to be stunned. He was an engineer, totally different personality than her. I hollered into the phone, "Are you nuts?" The whole floor went quiet.

After four years in Riverside, we moved back to San Diego. There, the marriage eventually ended and whatever I had accumulated monetarily was gone. Once stuck by me.

I began dating an engineer, also from the aircraft factory, and we had our problems. I swore to Once he was a louse; I would never date him again. When I had gone up to spend the night with Once, I changed my mind and went back to her house to get my clothes and stay with him. I found my clothes in a pile on her front steps! Again, Once stuck by me when that relationship eventually failed.

Once had a relationship I could only envy. He was funny, adventurous, and generous. He brought out the best in her. Their relationship was short-lived, but he passed after a valiant fight with cancer.

I had a lovely apartment in San Diego and was working for the Health Department, this time in a more prestigious position that fit my organizational skills and command of the English language. By now, I had gotten my stuff together and also had completed my course in Cursillo. I became a speaker at a couple weekends. I was a lector at San Diego Mission de Alcala and an RCIA sponsor.

Once and I loved to go to the Hometown Buffet and eat mostly ice cream and strawberries. If we didn't want to go out, we would buy Breyer's vanilla ice cream. I always swore I could eat an entire half gallon in one sitting. She kept daring me to do it. I never did. I wish I had.

Once would visit me often and was happy to be alone during the day. She would sit by the pool or on my small balcony and read her books. By now, she had the early stages of Parkinson's disease.

When Once was ready to return to her lovely apartment in Corona, California, she would hug me goodbye before I went to work. Most of the time, she would call me at work and ask, "Is it okay if I stay a couple more days?" And she did.

It came time to retire and live near my grandkids on the East Coast, after a successful stint with the County of San Diego. I had met a wonderful man and he, too, was going to move with me. We would marry in three months at his church back in El Cajon, California.

However, Once and I had planned a trip across the country, and I was determined to keep our plans. My intended husband was sorry to see us leave but took it in stride and stayed to have his house painted and sold.

The compressor went out in the car half a mile from the highway patrol station, just out of Barstow, and it was hot in the desert. Help was on the way quickly. Once was reaching in her underwear, and I asked her what the devil she was doing. She said, "I got money in here." I knew that she could be depended on, no matter the Parkinson's.

We spent a lot of time in the National Parks, visiting to see my friend Tres in Colorado Springs, time in South Dakota, and also Oklahoma City. Then, we stopped at Graceland to see Elvis's home. Once was the co-pilot and kept track of our route on our MapQuest books my new man had made for us. I only took one wrong turn, but that was because Once had fallen asleep.

When we returned to California for a couple of visits, Once's Parkinson's had progressed, but I never saw it go to the point where her sharp mind wasn't there. I kept in touch with her somewhat when she was in the "home," but not to a great extent, where she passed in June of 2020.

She was my buddy.

Numero Doce

"I'm going to be assertive...
If that's okay with you!"
— Think Again by Robert Anthony

I met Numero Doce during our stint on the San Diego County Deputy Sheriff's wives' group. This group was short lived but so essential to the well-being of the spouses who wait at home until the return of their partners so they can go to sleep.

We found time to help out at the sheriff's golf tournament by tooling around in a golf cart, selling beer. So what if I ran over a few frogs that got in our path? Sometimes we drove into places directly in the path of the golf balls. It was a dangerous job!

Eventually, we would both be divorced from the two sheriffs, but lucky to have gained our children from those marriages. Our friendship survived, and Doce and I spent long evenings on the phone. When we had time, we got together, especially with Doce's mom and aunts, who were a hoot! I even got to light the candles at some of their birthday parties. They would say, "Hey, somebody light the effing candles!"

I've lost count of which of us has been married the most, because one of Doce's marriages turned out to not be valid. She said, "We went on our honeymoon. He was married and I wasn't!"

Doce is so pretty and has a great education. She has had terrific government jobs. Therefore, she rubbed elbows with what I call "high rollers."

She was even married to a United States congressman (for a while). She usually has a man in her life.

Doce and I stay in touch, usually at Christmas, when I get her newsy letter. I also get letters from her daughter, who has given Doce some beautiful grandchildren.

Numero Trece and Lena

*"We all take different paths in life,
but no matter where we go,
we take a little of each other everywhere."*
— Tim McGraw

She was the friend who liked a clean house, to the point where it suited her best to entertain outside on the patio. That way, she could clean up the mess later and the house would stay spotless. Numero Trece appreciated a nice meal. She liked that I made it complete for my husband, including meat, potatoes, salad, and a dessert every night.

Trece wore a wig because she didn't want to be old, and she was outspoken. She was sitting in a rocker at Cuatro's house, and I was bent over, trying to explain how to bring up pictures on my cell phone. I talked louder because Trece was 99 years old at the time. After a few minutes, I could tell she really wasn't listening. She turned and said, "Uno! I'm not deaf!"

We were given a tour of her house (not allowed to sit down) because she wanted to show us that she had a *framed picture* of my Lena Yoskovitz character on her dining room display cabinet. Lena had appeared for my girlfriends at a restaurant a couple of times, and Trece was Lena's biggest fan.

Lena appeared mostly at my workplace. She would wander in at staff meetings or parties, confused, trying to find where she was and somewhat demented. Lena carried a JCPenney's or toilet paper bag with a few sheets of paper, or half of a bra hanging out of the bag. She always had a beautiful flower-brimmed hat and very thick eyeglasses. She also wore an old coat, buttoned askew, and a lovely scarf.

When Lena bent over to retrieve a list of things she needed to show or read to the folks, she would bend from the waist down with her rear end facing her audience.

The ladies in my office would practice dancing during our breaks at work, including our favorite, the Electric Slide. Seldom did they miss a chance to demonstrate their dance at an office party. Toward the end of the dance, Lena would join them, her hat flopping and eyeglasses bouncing.

When I turned 65 and everyone knew I was retiring, they gave me a bang-up surprise party. Lena's sisters were the main attraction. My boss even became one of Lena's sisters! I didn't recognize her at first until she came right up to me.

These were the good times.

Acknowledgments

A big *thank you* to my illustrator and grandson, Alexander, for his pictures to go with my "silly stories." His illustrations required him to read the stories and make matching pictures. I think he did a terrific job!

Thanks, also, to Ken Johnson, my "ever lovin'" husband who never hesitates to give me the time to write and positive feedback for my stories.

Lucy Bell, my dear friend since we were little girls jumping on the couch, and being best friends for life—thank you for being my critic.

About the Author

Always writing, Carol Owen Reynolds authors short stories just like many of you play golf, go fishing, or make crafts for your homes. The short stories that preceded her first book, *Stories from a North Dakota Cheerleader*, earned a letter of congratulations from Governor Doug Burgum after she took a chance and sent him a copy.

Putting thoughts into words was taught early on by her high school teacher, Elizabeth Pfeiffer. Later in life, Carol sought creative writing classes at Grossmont College in El Cajon, California.

This book, titled *The Locas*, is far different and more personal than her first book. It is a story about Carol's life before and after an awakening by the interference of a Catholic Cursillo. (In the Protestant faith, the program is called Walk to Emmaus.)

Your words of encouragement are welcome and can be sent to Jan-Carol Publishing at communications@jancarolpublishing.com.

www.ingramcontent.com/pod-product-compliance
Lightning Source LLC
Chambersburg PA
CBHW070451050426
42451CB00015B/3442